D0970065

MORE HERE
THAN LIGHT

More Here Than Light

New & Selected Poems

A. V. Christie

 The Ashland Poetry Press

Copyright © 2019 by the estate of A. V. Christie

All rights reserved. Except for brief quotations in critical reviews, this book, or parts thereof, must not be reproduced in any form without permission of the publisher. For further information, contact the Ashland Poetry Press, Ashland University, Ashland, OH 44805, www.ashlandpoetrypress.com.

Printed in the United States of America

ISBN: 978-0-912592-73-2

LCCN: 2019933595

Cover art: Chris Maynard, Featherfolio, LLC
Cover design:Nicholas Fedorchak

Author photo: Darcie Goldberg

Acknowledgments

In gratitude to the following publications which published versions of the poems in this book:

And I Began to Entertain Doubts was published as a chapbook in 2016 by Folded Word Press.

Man Dragged by Horse, Tumultuous River:
   Georgia Review: "And I Thought of Glass Flowers"
   Gettysburg Review: "Niagara"
   Missouri Review: "Corn Maze"
   New Ohio Review: "The Soul All Morning"
   Witness: "Ice Man"

The Wonders was published in 2014 as a chapbook from Seven Kitchens Press. Several sections of the poem appeared previously in *Poetry Northwest*.

Little Surrender:
   Blackbird: "Willingly" and "Outdoor Room"
   Cave Wall: "The Black Iris" and "Off the Solomon Islands"
   Cincinnati Review: "Scene"
   Commonweal: "Heart (2)" and "At Longwood Gardens"
   Crazyhorse: "In Here" and "Winter Afternoons"
   Poetry: "Foreword," "The Hen Swallows a Worm or Slug" and
         "Atmosphere"
   Southwest Review: "The Hollywood Finch"
   "The Hollywood Finch" also appeared in *The Breadloaf Anthology of New American Poets* edited by Michael Collier.

The Housing:
Poems in this book originally appeared in *Barrow Street, The Bread Loaf Anthology of New American Poets, Crazyhorse, Pleiades, Ploughshares, Poetry, Poetry Daily, Quarterly West, Seneca Review, Shenandoah.*

Nine Skies:

The American Scholar: "Liberty Print"

The Boston Review: "Alchemy," "Darwin Crosses the Andes," "Late Swim"

The City Paper: "Motion Study"

Ethos: "Into the Solid Air"

The Indiana Review: "In My Dream," "Legend," "Nine Skies"

The Iowa Review: "Coin," "Eye Brooch"

The Plum Review: "Your Harmonica"

Poetry Northwest: "Evermay-on-the-Delaware"

Sonora Review: "Their Titanic"

for my daughter
Gabriella Lyn Fattibene

and with gratitude to my many teachers, among them:
Elizabeth Spires, Eamon Grennan, Nancy Willard, Bill Gifford, John Aldrich Christie,
Michael Collier, Henri Cole, and Stanley Plumly

Contents

VII. Nine Skies

Except the Heaven had come so near—
So seemed to choose My Door—
The Distance would not haunt me so—
I had not hoped—before—
            —Emily Dickinson

Winter Miniature

for David

We speak of seeing the big picture.
But what of the little picture?
Size of a postage stamp:

snow melt
hastening, saying
in the ditch
a light-note—
what's more,
what's glorious,
reaching
all through you
suddenly.
High-gloss
on the far fields.
It's mine, my sun
flushed with evening,
my unmet, met—
kindred,
making her
languorous stretch
through cloud.
And he said
all one has to do
is make the miraculous
the norm.
I make of my thumbs
and forefingers
a little
view-finder-square-frame—

each ice bush
lit in it,
open to every light,
there's something

more here
than light,
and everything
shining with it.

I.

AND I BEGAN TO ENTERTAIN DOUBTS

And I Began to Entertain Doubts

(at The Museum of Medical Abnormalities)

Inside all the drawers of things swallowed—
and here is the woman turning to soap.

~

In this case, in this disorder,
a bruise creates bone, an incision, bone—biopsy,
                                        deep scrape,
                                        more bone.
The body's own beautiful secrets, scaffold:
needing no one.

~

At the body's command, cell by cell—

pain's profound alone-ness.

It was teeming.
It was about to teem.

~

Dull muscle that circulates. It seeds.
you have these far
reaches in you—

whole factions of capillaries.

~

Ribs fuse, a type of healing,
Pelvis heals into a hard, white page—
                                a felt concavity.

The body something that holds
These thousand elaborate joinings.

~

Some believe the body has three souls:

The one at the heart, it goes heavenward.

The soul in the arm—the pulse—
The soul in the head or neck—the artery—

these stay to become the bodies of beasts
or an anatomical condition.

~

Incursions and/or excursions
lesions
uptake, a mass—

bone dot net.

~

Body Magic, Adventure Room
the splitting and doubling—
The Epilogue

Hidden: underside of a swan's wing, there where
    it's very strict and ongoing.

~

The Physic garden
at Royal Hospital Road
and Swan Walk

        is thriving on its southerly aspect.

The fernery
and the Garden of Useful Plants:
here, where apothecaries extracted compounds
that went on to become, even now, my killing,
healing agents.

The glass house,
Spanish moss and metaphysics—
thick in the air, being and knowing, causes and time.

~

It's rare to see roses in poems anymore.

And what have the thorns become?
I will be the thorn.

~

This was almost a poem with no bird in it. Medicinal.
Those are not questions you get to know the answers of.

~

While my body is making tiny alterations, my
x-husband tears out a photo of an infinity pool
from *Architectural Digest* and puts it on his vision
board.

~

I advance: a ruin, an amalgam, a tracery—
    wound-connected—a grievance.
Blood came from my nipple.

~

I began to entertain doubts about the trees
around the house, and even about the faucets
through which the water ran...

~

A housed-in animal
An *engagé*
in the form of a white moth so as not to show itself.

~

Slow   Slow   Slow   Slow   Slow

~

Late-summer wasps are startlingly mean,
the hive teeming.

(Some self-help book telling me there's honey——.)

Having cancer at midnight and doing a Brazilian.
He'll not be here. No cold cloth.
We'd known that.

Each of us, this frail cell
made separate from the next.

Yet, there is a persistence.

~

The jaw locks up in its concentration:
                                    shears that cut into color.

You see the tack marks of other possibilities
layerings, pencil marks, a technique kept secret.

White standing for man and woman.

I am annulled.
            No. Not any.

~

Let me be dramatic and say death is my
    second skeleton.
It listens while others make their plans.

What is pinned up, shifts in the room
of comings and goings.

~

Consider the free Bible download.
Re-consider the morning song of praise.

~

Sometimes the grit becomes a pearl, a bright spot.

~

And he began to come around again and she held
    the possibility like lake water
her cupped hands, it was subtle, this returning—
    it did or did not happen.

~

It was, too, the death of the magnolia year,
    I'd been kicked off my land.
It could rain blood for all I cared.

My whole untidy life, and
the girl playing in the next yard, all she did
    was scream—.
It was her only language.

~

Some women separate eggs in the palm of their hands.

~

Shortness of breath—
what a palm holds, what a cabinet holds, what a
    room holds, what a breath holds. An idea
that held.

Bereft and bereaved.
What a sky can hold: the rising up in it and all that
    falls.

~

Did I ever stand here
with a lantern?
with an owl's call?

~

They cry out for an offering of flowers or fruit.

~

The stricken one turns out to be something else
    altogether,
and is changed back.

~

The Knife Thrower aimed at what he thought
was a complicated leaf—acanthus?—
cut from paper,

but really it was her strange-patterned heart.

What is missing might be affixed somewhere else
    in the composition.
His body was all knife.

~

Poor woman in the waiting room
thought the blood flowing so dark, so
bright from her might be a renewal—
O, to be again
          desirable

but it was disease pulling out of her
all that was in her.

~

Consider the halt in the night:
White waiting, a white hour, a little month.

Cause means that from which a thing comes into
being, e.g., the bronze of the statue, the silver of the
saucer and the classes which include these.

~

I fold the paper in half:
On this side what's disobedient—
On this side what is extensive—
Pain here and here,
          bones ticking, ticking
          and alight.

One of the last organs, size of a fist.

~

It is December.
Time now to use the words and imagery,
use up the raw materials.

II.

UNCOLLECTED POEMS

And I Thought of the Procedure

This Friday while they are laying new track after the wreck,
I wonder what laying new track looks like.
And I am meticulously picking lint and cat-hair off my daughter's cardigan,
        which is black.
But mostly, I am making a study of my body. Could words save me?

Words like density and avid have been handed back to me changed
now, and palpable.

I have mosaic attenuations in my lungs—
I don't care what this means. There are findings, shadowings.
The breast's 11 o'clock centimeters and millimeters.
Could my whole body give way to words? What procedure
would allow this? What appropriate action taken
so I could recover into 17 more pages of the hushed-marrow poem?

I present myself for staging, I take off my blouse—
        wrongful, clavicle, proximal, scan
        caudal, residual, partial, enhance
Into my veins
        ilium, axial, sternum, respond
The eyes close to
authorize, delineate, viable, spine
an ether, a swimming
mid-thigh comparison, dilute, defined
inward thoughts and wanderings
a shoulder, a prior study, a technique, an assay
to places
lytic, lobe, coronal, pelvic
A darkening
release, node, mild and diffuse

wholly suggestive of an entity, a guide.

I undergo—

Poem in Which I Burn the Remaining Coffee Filters

So huge, the moon—indulgent, almost literary.
I am feeling every wound or mistake as it turns to bone—
is cast at the foundry or machined.

I had said I wondered what would be happening
at the end, 500 of them, at the last coffee filter.
Maybe the box I hold now holds 500 matches,
I don't know.

Walking along the aisles of the grocery store
I'd felt like kicking almost everything over.

Midway through the coffee filters,
here this disease was happening to me; it crowded in.

I couldn't stand the way the coffee filters sat there
in a neat, determined stack, folded together
white in accordion folds
like the fans I made out of paper in elementary school.

And yet, in this life, much beauty had seemed to arrive,
sought me. And I had loved
through all this carrying on.

Let me say, coffee filters do not burn well,
but I am almost through, am dogged,
tossing a few at a time into the terra cotta plant pot
out on my back porch.

I am under this patient, inconstant stay of the moon—
this or that god damn blood or blue or
harvest moon.

The filters, they are smoldering slowly along the edges,
looking like moments, or lit coral,
looking to me like a sort of-unthinkable, stirring flower.

The Gulls of Dublin

They surprise me, their being here
    They speak, speak
    of new truths and false beliefs

I have traveled from one island to another,
    from a turn of events.
    Where is my ground?
    And what have I come to say?

Gulls can see sharply, can see great distances.
    From where can I speak?
    From what can I extrapolate—?
    bonework, a vigilance, a parting of leaves.

I, too, am capable of many voices, tones,
    pressing if not transformative calls—.
    I open the small blue box in my throat.
    I try to see around me widely.

They know I want to speak; they would include me
    in their speech. They know of bodies,
    of crusaders—their leathery hands—
    of ghosts, and lavender, and priests.

They've taken bread from the palm of a child
    whose birth caused the death of her mother.
    They know I have my own body, that I stayed
    awake with it days before it was changed.

They know I speak as one changed.

I see they cover the whole city—inner
          and otherwise. They remind me
          from their point of view that everything
          is profusion, and none of it is him.

They say to me I am essential. They remark
          on my soul, teeming and bright, I see it as encumbered, they see it
          which I don't see.

They have not heard of the ship on fire
          that turned into the wind. But they do know
          about the ghostly ship from Japan,
          the rusted-bleeding vessel Ryou-Un Maru
          adrift for a year in open seas.

I wonder what postulates they live by
          these gulls, circling and landing—
          circling and landing—.

Their voices are not God's, although harsh.
          I know this because I bought online,
          for $19.95, *5 Steps to Hearing God's Voice.*

One has to walk right into the center of things.

My heart's compressed to a tumor
          and the gulls are not interested in me
          in any mythical way.

They know I'm not proud of wanting a hole in him
      the shape of me.
      They can laugh that off, but I can't.
      I've always had this disease.

It is, isn't it, the speaking disease.
      Each day now, the gulls and I, we fly
      well past sunset.

Above the city, we are humble,   we prevail,
      I've learned one doesn't need a vast message
      to call out—

Idea: Control

Was another's body / not like some bright / obstruction?
—Carol Frost

The necessary drips in and burns at times.
The future stands on so much air, as it always has.
Pure idea, write the poem that's pure idea.
Without décor.
           Daily you wake, your will asserts
itself, crystallizes, gestures. Again.
All recommences and is managed.
This becomes collecting one's thoughts—
what's causal, distinctions drawn, further
refinements. Stays.
The unclarified clarified and complete—
it's lawful-seeming, and all of it holds.
How many ways can one say it? You're a master.
You fabricate, enclose.
So much that must first ask your permission.

You will find that what is left is bent and clean,
that all is still, that the outcome is stillness.

Idea: Ire

It is the narrowest house on earth:
48 inches in width.
One is aware of its size
at every turn.
　　You must take a ladder
to where you can be fed,
where someone can put balm to your lips,
hold your fierce hands in their hands.
Where you can be put gently to bed.

Oh, bitterness after shining bitterness:
　　a varnish.

Your heart—what have you got?
Small talk, a thread, stem of a vivid cherry,
a wish you are trying to remember.
Your anger, how it assails every corner
here
　　so punishingly, so accomplished.

III.

MAN DRAGGED BY HORSE, TUMULTUOUS RIVER

Corn Maze

I heard the next voice over:
Think *small* it said. *Think small.*
Through the halls, the walls of corn,
I heard how the voice was held together
by its heritage of fear
and an inescapable sound of wings.
I had tried also always to flee—
the desire that rises and falters unceremoniously
Now I was in the middle with a tall flag
and a poor diagram shedding no light,
crosshatched hay strewn on the path.
It felt as though we all were the remnant
of some great trauma. Wandering.
One voice later, at the two hour mark,
I heard a father: *Shut up or I'll rip your tongue out.*
This was maybe too near the center part of our map.
(Where we'd come to again.)
And I'd been one who'd tried always to position
herself at the edge of a field.
I thought we would simply go in and come out.
But here was density, tunnels leading back
to a childhood, its basic cosmology of annihilation.
Oh, this rustling and reliable sequence
of panic—I wondered who could I really be
without it?

On Longing

My body is the souvenir
haunting like the bracelet of dimes
at the junk store belonging to
and unhinged from a narrative, brought down
beside the frame in which trimmed,
crimped paper makes a dear bachelor button,
marigold, forget-me-not
bouquet—the body shining or shameful, the body tarnished,
patronized, pitied, wronged,
trying to say itself, something
of itself—
I was his I was hers I was his again
into all the silence here.
And why would miniatures be any simpler:
little hatbox, tiny pencil,
little silhouette, minute Victorian lamppost

the painstaking ship in a bottle—
any small story
withheld, intact.

Address to the Sun

after a Nigerian tale

Sun. Sun. I am the water. Remember once
we'd lived as friends, together,
side by side on the Earth.

You'd visit, you'd reach
out to me your lit hands.
Then you invited me. I declined. You invited,
Water: I will take you into my house,
you said. I was teeming and knew
your house could not hold
me. You tried and sometimes tried again to build
what might allow for something so huge.
How to complete it? I spilled
in, pulled, was tidal. Very soon I was knee-deep.
I was the height of men when
you began to know better. You took then
to the topmost, utmost crow's nest of the truth.
I surged in—o whalebone!—and watched
a house succumb. House gone under
a wave and you safe in the unavailable,
unassailable sky.

Allure

And I can feel it, the going still further—
see the beckoning arc, sunlit, of the deer's
long neck come to rest at the road's shoulder.
Yearning, pale—like a woman's neck and throat in pleasure.
I had thought what I sought was pleasure.
Further, the deer's ribs have been picked clean—a lyre
Here, it would seem is my music—so lovely, dire.
To be thus destroyed, left, used up by a lover.
Then to drag what's sharp across skin, over
Top of the heart's unsteady endeavor,
Its dull whisper, waver, murmur, never.
One feels in one's self, in the hour,
A before and before and before,
An inner lateness—a whir and structure.

And I Thought of Armor

And I thought of armor, the deep-set
heart, the whole history of fortification.
The first wooden shield.

Here is the tapestry in which the warriors lean in.
Lover and assailant.

Armor, amour,
the clamor, the clambering out of the blue-black weight—
the word *cuisse* almost as beautiful
as the inner thigh it protects.

Here is my vital throat, fragile cheek—.
The wolf's teeth pattern.
Temper me, hinder, anneal, heal.

In armor, anything
I'd touch is armored.

And the weapons also advance—
the capabilities, the keeping pace with
love or some other edged weapon.

It could be beautiful—fluted, flanged, ridged, embossed,
upswept, with foliage, medallions—
to reach for you.

Quick glimpse of something
glancing and enameled, with a tell-tale shine—I know it.

But quick, too, it's back to what's best—
to tactics, a decoration skilled yet subdued.

The Painters Have Gone

have taken their singing, taken the taking off
of their shirts away to a far address.

How they brought me to myself.

The other women, their yellow gloves
for cleaning, their garden gloves.
No to the elements, they say.
And then again, *No*.

I want the dirt's tilth—to feel it, break it
down in my hands as it breaks my hands down.
Washing the dishes I rely on the cup's edge
like an unearthed bone.

We lose everything.

I had a dream when the painters left:
I had perfectly spent my body.
In my tomb near the flurry
of where my head might have been
                    two translucent wine jars as tall as I was.

Ice Man

What hath not man sought out and found
But his dear God?
—George Herbert

We approach you, sir, interrogate
your origins & migrations—
                    glacier watershed alpine
Glacier man, mummy,
ice man, copper-age man, window.
Arms & legs.

We find in your digestive tract traces
of mosses, pollen.

Reading strontium & lead (we can read these)
and the more stable carbon, we wrest
from you ongoing intelligence.

Mica ages in your intestines.
White mica, three micas, seven micas—
                    molecular analysis demonstrates
your neolithic trustworthiness.

Isotopic study & we get at you,
move you in our minds from here to there.

We probe all your archive.

A valley's half-life—
we pinpoint your biomineral range,
your materials & potential
                    gneisses limestone volcanics
From basalts, your integrated value.

Nomad, itinerant man,
we see that you grind your cereal.

You've ingested the grinding rock.

　　　　We've ascertained your saliva: base
　　　　as it worked away at the outermost
　　　　primitive enamel.

Even the waters you drank　　*ice melt*
snow melt　　melt-water deep in your cortical femur
we systematically reconstruct.

We know the contributions, alterations,
　　　　　　　　　　　　　　　　what hurt.

One of the no-names, sir, *monstrous forms*
And lives with which we have nothing, we like
To hope, in common.

Resolvable, finally, to conclusory statements—

Our Mr. Sampling
Our Mr. Therefore

The Soul All Morning

It selects. It speaks.
It can take the stars,
can draw back.
Some say it is constrained—.
It quarrels, it rejects.
Mine somehow sometimes
slips out, goes and goes
delicate-filmed.
It wields, then feels fragile.
It likens itself to,
refutes sin.
It wakes and wanders the light
across water, a ripple.
Does it tremble or no?
I tend, cajole.
It prefers to hide
hundreds of feet back
from the main road.
I am the main road.

Decline

To get here, the knocking steam, coursing
rust of the whole system, overflow
valve of it, the pinhole leak
a minute weakness at work
in the walls, saturating—runnels
and the ceiling bubbling.
Before the door is swollen shut,
the new titrate, departure
of the poet, everything walking
back and forth upon dread
and clicking. Wind that takes
a house down. Already in March
reading Job. Prior to which
one deer, just one
having been put at close-range
from its misery
out the perfect frame
of the front window. This allowed
the piece of advice,
straying along a baseboard,
the skittering constancy
of assassins and suicides.
In order to get here:
to be the lone object in a room
upon which
the whetted night comes.

Man Dragged by Horse, Tumultuous River

house hit by lightning

an attack at the crossroads

woman & son in hospital

hole in my side

woman kneels with candle

man kneels with candle

o, Lady of light, my

infinite thanks

girl recovers

taken ill with eruptions

the low & lowering dream

girl recovers from heart malady

afraid of death

afraid of terrible life

this cart accident

please I give my whole heart

these clouds and cross

8000 lightning strikes

touch off 800 fires

child recovers from mysterious occurrence

boy stuck between two rocks

baby cured of smallpox

man recovers stolen livestock

man with shooting pains to the head

a serious internal affliction

an entreaty, a blood illness

a miracle, this

Your generosity and favor

neighbor girl washed away by river

Ex Votos

after Frida Kahlo

There'd been a full hemorrhage of blood,
a floating bed, pelvic bone, and time
moved—*soft covered open*—like a snail off
toward the factories of the horizon

~

I had been broken open, the world wore its stone mask
there was a Blue House in a church of cloud in one corner
there was a cactus fence

~

Dead-winged—my heart I thought too hot
or caustic so lace dissolved away from it
and I held my own hand

~

Life pierced with its immense look, its marigolds
and ravines, its far-reaching stain and corset

I was not to be brightened
by any lovebird or flower

~

To be one fractured column
wearing affliction's own thorn necklace

To sleep in a canopy-bed all made of bones

~

I painted how it was:
excruciating shine on the surgical clamp
apple at about heart-height, progress
of the suicide out of the frame

I tried to paint what held it all together:
the vines, veins—the blood and ribbon

Niagara

She is at the edge of, the broken, the smooth, the no-moment-the-same,
the noise, the force, the forced.

She is afraid of analogies: *it could be anything.*
My daughter has started to become alone.
In the mist: cormorants.

Metaphor is one damn flimsy ineffectual barrel off the edge of.
It's got nothing on grief, the sheer scale of it, tumult,
and the going under.

Metaphor pretends to be vast and is an embarrassment.

So many cataclysms
any of which can introduce a double-ness into life.
To make a view larger or smaller.
All the ways to say *Help me, Help me.*

So many syndromes one after the other
Am I alive or dead?
Is this a dream or an afterlife?
Has the blood turned to powder?
No continuing recognition of my face—
no corresponding self.

And, too, I read about the experiential seizure—
always the vision, while convulsing, before going down:
repeatedly, guttering of the city in ruins
or watching people enter the room
with snow on their clothes.

No sense—so that
99¢ dreams are to breathtaking
as again and again is to wind

body is to threshold   as fear not is to torrent
gesture is to disturbance   as imply is to sunset.

Thus it follows, dear one, thus—and thus—.

Love is this thundering veil, this vast span
with and without precedent.

Amish Country

for the schoolgirls

A blue day asking forgiveness. My daughter and I have been making
a colonial dress with print apron. It is a large skirt—gentle, gentle
at the gathering. I press the darts of her bodice. Seams.
The lace is running through my hands. I've not used these words—
this word selvage for edge—in a long time. After a trip to Amish Country
my sister had sewn for her daughter an Amish bonnet— she'd used doubled white
organza light like a yesterday whisper and spray starch. The moon
puts a hem to the clouds. Sometimes there seems a language for everything.
Other times only silence: swallows nesting in the turned under shadow
of the eaves of the schoolhouse. Silence under the thin lids of canned peaches.
Silence now of the meadow without a school. And there will be long sermons.

I know the small chest as cave, its breathless ladder of fear.
I will tell you, too—it is beautiful, inviolate.

It is a large skirt my daughter and I have been making.
I am hurrying.

Self-Help Exercise

*Name 3 things you're grateful for today and perhaps what you have done to bring
them into your life.*

In gratitude for the dogwood buds letting go just in time
and all that I've learned to make bud up in my persisting hands

and to the peepers: I have spent whole nights blowing into your mouths
that air so you can play out—you little perpetual, tin-night, wind-up night

machines. I take responsibility for today's breadth of green
that comes somehow to instruct, for Prettyboy Dam, the accord of light
along a dam's rim, siren-sheen of the mallard's head.

I've made the red-tail visit low over the side yard, have honed today
its beak, making the mourning dove's breast softer to meet it—

shells of the turtles basking in sun I've achieved, hammered thin that dark
to give some warmth and the partially sunken tree limb they've climbed

I can be said to have made the elm, made it succumb
Into my hollowed basin, filled to become the backwoods pond.
What have I not done?

I've restored here the snake's sun-struck enamel, the oriole's piercing
song—
sweet central concern and clear cousin to the clear-down-to-the-source

ongoing spring: look: in the waters a constant pale grit sent up
from the deep center purity of what I have made. I diversify, dismiss

all antecedents. I pursue the mass of things, pursue a strength—
the whole apparatus and assembly, that clack of grasshopper motif.
Called for the delicate fixture of the deer's lit-at-dusk tail.

The deer will give its consummate blood across four lanes of the interstate
as each granite erratic is strewn, my insistent glacier, ensouled,

it adjusts purely, constantly, is sustained. I am at work now
adjusting a sky that does not collapse of its own weight.

And I Thought of Glass Flowers

Some say superior people disdain the glass flowers at Harvard,
and so I sought the flowers out.
Arrayed they were, in low light, in glass cases.

I cried unexpectedly at their glass roots, cried
at the beauty of the task:
transverse section, frond, pod, stamen, thousands
of botanical specimens made to hold still.

And I felt there was, too, something unlawful about it.
      Where there was first an iris, an iris to the touch,
      there was now a glass iris—.
Now loss. Now triumph.

And I saw that
laid open, every song is a love song.

IV.

THE WONDERS

The Wonders

Indeed, in all these surviving records, in each and every tongue, written in the century and a half or so following Nebuchadnessar's death in 562 BC, there is no mention at all of Hanging Gardens in Babylon.
—*John and Elizabeth Romer*

Be the voice of night and Florida in my ear.
—*Wallace Stevens*

I believed in you.
I believed there was a vicinity
where hope and the colossal
left its residue. That it was love.
That it was ambition.
That there were walls there.
A city gate. A dynasty in the desert
in bottlebrush and apricot
for a queen, a wife.
That hung down its excess
and perfumes, was
a wonder—part human wonder—
of the world.

~

Here is your mountain, its ramparts—
what I have fortified vastly
for you.
          Here is your heroic king.
And bitumen to hold this dream
together, vaults and arches
each brick baked in sun
in the month of bricks.
Our water spirals up
from the Euphrates and from
these orchards the massive timber
for boats, for our city gates.

Laden, and all
its enclosures.

If you come, come in manuscript,
if you come.

~

Embroidered in
where shadows would be—peacocks.
Pheasants curl in your lap,
the gorgeous splitting open
of pomegranates. Oldest dream
of a place: I put a stone in my mouth
for its sweetness.
        Where each tree
is a type of workshop. Tall and watchful,
evergreen, evergreen —.

Even the grass's frail membrane is honeyed.

~

These trees—
such roots as to form a ceiling,
but loosely
to let the stars through.
Is this a place that goes too far?
Oysters and nectar, an incense
so pleasurable and potent
it turns our hair gray. I'll eat
this, continuously.
I had been starving, some long
dragging at my throat, here
each shrub is hung with amethyst.

~

This garden rooted in air
in error and mistranslation.
My Hanging Gardens. Possibly
you grew more ornamented
from a closely allied word
for simple terracing:
necessity of the desert,
the worked-at inundation.
    Now   *All your heart could desire*
becomes thin and perhaps
no place to be excavated
for its complex of waterfalls—
mirage, bitumen, the irrigating
passageways.

Not a hoax, exactly,
just as the fairy tale is not.
Just radiant bulwark
made of what's insubstantial;

little surrender, richly perfumed.

~

To be clear, such a garden
grows from slavery, from capture,
is built up from plunder, blood
orchards as souvenir, the sissoo,
terebinth, nightshade,
prickly cedar
brought home with care
from collecting trips across Persia.
The rare and delicate wonders,
the marauders:
I built a pillar by the city gate, flayed
all the chiefs and covered the pillar
with skin. I made one pillar
of the living and another of heads.

Star thistle, papaver, the golden section,
the Persian White—some seed
heads hold ten thousand seeds.

~

Ponderous, my imaginings
        the bruisy figs

and obelisks
apricots, armies
I am cultivating:
a mind is this shady grove
and I am its gardener.

I grasp at
    the roots of paradise.

It's skillful work
building any wonder.

~

And we were powerless—
we pulled our nutriment
from air, from
an image.

Now forgetting is essential.

~

The Biblical garden.

Scholars map out
so many paces of hearsay
along one side.

They grow more sure.
The model for Eden,
that come-slowly paradise.

Little crockery shard.

Eden that opened
in a desert,
throats of orchids and dusks
and flutes, the clotting up
with canna's flame-spires and date palms,
unfurling fronds in the time-lapse
of documentaries, diffuse and lit
as exaggerations are
passed down, copied out
document to document
in rumors of trees

and the few shadows playing along.

~

They build this city all over again,
its bitter river.

There were rings
made of silver, to store silver.

Forty feet down, the door's
still locked, its dusty bolt.

Cut a new doorway.

Rib-section of an animal.
Fragment by fragment
they split the bird open—
vinegar, mint, salt.

~

The gardens recede, the dampened roots—
swift falcon past pear and olive,
past gates
the processional roads
and grandest phases
Something exists to the north,
prosaic and with difficulty.
The grapes buttressed
hidden somewhere
in the plans of Babylon.
A garden of two springs
for the shedding of blossom.

Unlikely, and the downward
force of all those roots.

~

You attacked like a storm.
Overthrew.
As the winds proceed—
roofs then foundation—.
You ravaged, did not spare.
Even the dust you took off
in a jar.

~

I daub my eyes with kohl
from a mussel shell, a color
called *let him come let him come.*

~

From wonder
to mistake
through etymology
or paradise

through all that's precious
the close hennaed flesh—
to succumb and succumb.

~

Bring honey from dates and tell me it's mountain honey, red honey.
Press fruit into cake, touch meat with fire.

~

It was wondrous, I say,
wondrous.

Here, in wet clay, with sharp
pick and reed's prick,
is where error makes its blunt-end mark.

Then force, brow-beat
the shrubs.

~

Today I am a believer again
        in imported trees
        whose leaves won't tire;
        in gold mines, figs, and gold-mining
        ants; in the land without shadows;
        a snake's sugary urine
        that burns the skin.
        No part of my ideal has been plundered,
        undone. Today
        I excavate the panoply.

        I will show how the pillars of stone
        support more than a fiction.
        What I say will be shown
        to be trustworthy, enduring,

sturdy——an ox of the verbal.
I will prove the golden whores, will find
the traveler's account, prove

this idea like a hundred proven gods.
It was no scarlet, broad-leaved dream.

I will show you the aqueducts.
I will show you the apotheosis.

~

Trellis of *what now*
in the pleasure garden.
I make to myself
the sound of water.

If hanging means terraced
then a fountain is a furrow
a fern is a thirst
the stars are throats
and songs are seeds.

If fallen means expanse
then rain is a tide
and rampart means a dry spell
an orchid is sand
the garden is reeds.

If season means sister
and branch means queen
then declination means storm.

The fuchsias devolve.
Olives dissemble.

And desire, there
Is no such animal——.
And the door stands open.

~

V.

LITTLE SURRENDER

In Here

I like the certain timbre of a zealot's voice
someone's in charge, this does
go deep in me.
I like tapping the barometer.
I like burying the mourning dove, amber
chrysanthemums for her breast, and the way
the white horse goes sudden from standing,
down on the hard election-year ground
to rub its back, move its legs in the air.
I like the tensed thrill of having a nemesis.
I like to think that where my lungs should be
there is a cavern, reaching way back
and beneath a ledge
I can feel when I want something.
I like the pond as an eye that looks up,
its glance that wavers in here
on the ceiling.

Heart (2)

The heart is an old man mouthing obscenities.
Muttering, muttering.
On the echo monitor each beat becomes
an aurora borealis, and the valve
flaps like the top of an old cartoon stovepipe.
You house these tunnels—
put your dark head down and enter.
Now the rhythm's colorized, vivid
like weather on the 6 o'clock news:
the front moves, flashes, subsides.
You have been vigilant.
On the sonogram the child-heart was
a little cricket muscle. Did you guess
hearts grow pitiless or monstrous
in such grainy, uncanny mineshafts as this?

The Black Iris

It is night, a fox at the edges.
This would be the time to steal the black iris
from the foundation plantings
of the building set for demolition.
For days I've been laboring
in the shadow of this idea.
It's envy. And the iris is not a genuine black.
Life is hiding its riches from me—
all to itself like a trumpet impresario
covering the glories
of his finger work beneath a handkerchief.
Each day I talk myself out of having
the black iris. I want it.
I consider, reconsider in ways
all the blunt, sure days do not.
This ugly, knotted, fibrous corm:
it spreads in me, might sustain.
I hear the fox move off—such a wail,
taking the night in its possession.

Foreword

I was conceived in the cruelest month
in whatever spring California could muster.
A little rain—with some more likely.
And the buckeyes were they yet on the ground?
Damn my father's smooth stone eyes,
other prevailing enticements and what Eliot called
the *female stench*. Damn the oaks,
their histrionics, struggling in the fog.
Spider webs lay in the grass, misted
and looking like misspent galaxies.
I cry into and out of this moment.
Pound told Eliot: strike this and this.
What was weak got dropped, and the poem
stood stronger without it.

Atmosphere

The canals of Mars
beseech various oxides, vast
dust storms
of a dulled red,
a daytime warmth
that only reaches so far.

Let's call these fissures canals
so we'll think of Venice
looking through our telescope
as Mars comes this close

in this our anniversary year
with its thin atmosphere
and, to be probed,
its extreme cold.

The Hen Swallows a Worm or Slug

We scratch at the backyard together
through leaf mould, worm casings she kicks off
in a fan behind her. I use a stick
to dig, to find for her what she's shown me
near the roots, at the edge of a step—sticky
slug on the underside of a hosta's leaf.
How complicated she is and how resigned.
Between her beak and my outstretched hand,
the worm's writhing. Then the long slick going
down. It fills the throat, like all that's swallowed.
     Her head chucks it back,
     for the worm again dark.
     The hen's pupil dilates.
     She wends and follows.

Her queries, sighs, low gurgles, the hastening
click of her nails on pavement then hungry
again into the grass. Grubs are larger
than pale yellow larvae I prise from inside
chestnuts. These mucousy blind wanderers
she eats right from my palm. Nevertheless I am
repulsed by my husband's embrace. I turn
now from his thick belly, breasts, his interests.
A body I had clambered over, loved.
I scrabble, struggle. I cover myself.
     Another sticky truth dug up
     that I must re-bury—
     sorry on hands and knees,
     hungry and wary.

Winter Afternoons

The storm is upon us.
The wind. November trees,
the stand of them pitching—
branches thickly superimposed.
Lithe, lithe. All pleasure
has left our bodies.
Starlings blown
across the swift marionette sky
and light-wrack on corn stubble.

Light that collapses time.

Same rake tines at the fence posts.
Same leaves—reassembled—
and on to their same moldering.
Same left at the stop sign. The cold,
the shortness of breath.
Nests clotting up in the branches.
Same "slant of light" in the poem.

And these taken together are the spell.

Do commence,
commence the fairy tale.

It's not the children who will be in need of it.

Willingly

There is a little world in the bird's mind budding open,
a world made from watching and the sound of the rasp
making things still smaller—the door, the window frame.
Here they speak of a purse with buttons across its flap
that costs a great sum: cold button, sky button, goldenrod
and hurt buttons, suet and sun. Here she reads aloud
a poem about a woman who becomes a fish
for a man, who lies down on her belly to be cooked
on the heat-ridden stones. And this, as the garden figurine falls
willingly into the impatiens. And comes something about a child
but the fluster of it—what rips—subsides. Little world
where squirrels are struck, the bounty now of what's hidden.
And the cat sends its purr out enlarging to become
the jet that rumbles night high up over the mid-Atlantic states.
This world—the bird's wide infinite—lived out
one tiny, overseen thought at a time.

On a Cruise Ship

The moth out at sea, the floating weed
only one person sees their few moments
of observable story, their scale.
Distance in all directions and time—
we go forward into more forward,
into a blue we had only suspected.
I lay my whole body down on the deck
In order to feel the pitch, the implications.
Such a vast sadness.
The bow of a boat must be made from trust or belief.
Many are assuaged each morning by our coordinates.
At night all these nautical miles out, the sea
spreads out for me its far-reaching theories.
I hold tight to the fine wooden rail: feel the sea
how it wants to include me.

Scene

In the jewel-box theater, the marionette Oberon has goat's legs
and a peacock tail that fans out in the planning.

The lovers awake. I am awakened.

Awakened and diffuse, hammered thin like precious metal.

Awake like the beck cabbage that unfurls, covers the bank entirely
in a bright week.

A dissipation, all surface area to summer's edge
so that each sentence can delve and trance, is hooved, devoted.

I am in play, let loose

to the beckoning
and shaded spots where the mild eddying and expansion is.

It's the tryst, the gorgeous thought, its shock taken in
all down and through.

Each scene, I know, will with time cohere
and dim. I'll be the one unstrung

and central to this shimmer of error.

The Hollywood Finch

I thought someone had said Olmsted brought them
east to brighten the edge, finish
with a peripheral and brief red
his Central Park. But here, a few pages past
the Ash-throated Flycatcher, Dark-eyed
Junco, I read of the modest and ruddy House Finch
whom California cage-bird dealers dubbed
"Hollywood" and, in 1940, shipped in a purplish,
illegal scheme to New York. Fearing violations,
fines, the store clerks of Manhattan
released the birds which spread to Long Island
survived north to Connecticut and south
to Maryland where this morning I watched them
flicking suet in the angled sun. And I thought
to myself in the early hush—how tenuous
and grandiose are the plans, how small
these beaks eating the seed of the brittlebush.

What to Make of It

An artist of spare room or corner or pasture, in soot
and spit, in lavished overcast perspective. How
it went together, how it did and undid. He hid
his bundled work in the barn, balanced on a beam
exactly midway in that dark.

No one wrote of the target of an eye,
the host, the marrow, the monosyllable the way
she could write.

The crow flies with a pale straw in its beak.

Why always the suggestion— a molestation
or bastard brother who killed himself.

I heard of a little girl afraid to go out in the wind.
Leave her alone.
Don't tell me any more about her.

Hen

Isn't it everything the way you gather
        your foot back,
        pull it delicate-
        ly up before each step.

The precision of your beak,
        the quick quick to each
        thistle-seed.

My whole world
        in your amber eye
        poised, tipped
        up as you drink.

The look to all kinds of heaven.

You roost outside in everything
        and the joists, struts
        of each merciless hour
        loosen. Your neck spills
        these feathered rusts.

I'm amazed to think
        next to the blink of your eye
        a man is nothing——.

And the color of even one
        of your eggs is so far
        beyond the reach of
        any day-laboring poem.

Outdoor Room

There was a rubber band in me
you plucked and it would pluck and hammer
as I waited in the dark, any breeze
that was from the window
to relax in order to drive home—
jittery, to come down, pull my limbs
                              together.

Those high, hot days—the air, more of it
up there. Then again night, the pool lit.
A ready thing. You'd bring out the mattress,
breathe at the nape of my neck
& I'd go all slick and guttering.
We were young then when the oaks watched
you ruin me with attention.

Off the Solomon Islands

War wrecks beneath the shut-seeming sea,
under wing the wrasse and sweet lips haunt the current,
a moon signals corals to spawn.
More tree coral's tender colored bloom.
More brain coral.
More freight of glorious rosettes.
More bombs at fifteen-second intervals.
Jellyfish drift in, inhabit for a time the engine room—
easy, and little left to fear.

The enemy, tracer-fire wane in feather stars
inching along the battered propeller.
Hundreds of feet down grouper, a tank, solitary P-51 upright,
such formations.

What will corrode and what harden here.
What can flourish.

The narrator discusses how ruin can be
an architecture, basis for a reef, can become
(he uses the living word) *a backbone*.

And the words *gunner, redoubt, ordnance*
are pulled back into the mouths
of the barrel sponge.

At Longwood Gardens

Here there is one sycamore propped.

Propped with timbers as big, bigger
than the tree's limbs.
Such polished, weathered crutches.
It is this caring that touches.
One can imagine the design on graph paper.
At the pleasure garden,
midst the beardstongue, the quince,
and tower of jewels,

the tree stumbled and was put back.

It stumbled beside a glory of copper beech
and found the orchids exhausting,
like too many lives — spotted or spiked—
their stylized drooping mustaches
from an ancient Chinese print.

The sycamore stumbled and was put back up.

VI.

THE HOUSING

Dusk and the Wife

                              in with the child
who drops like a weighted lure,
flashes down, down to sleep.
The husband suburban, pulls up
a bright folder called Taxes
in the coming dark (his young
coworker in Baja, her unfettered
surface away on vacation).

In the coming dark the grey
squirrel ripples across outside
time-lapse.

So many leaves to the trees
this many   this many

              What is it then?

He opens to the red head, her
pale pink mesh demi
embroidered, pulled down
taut strap hard pressed
to hold the gorgeous half-spill
lit access of breast.
She slightly bites her lip
while the wife half a dream away
is pressed by his good friend
against a building. They could be
in Florence—all these angels.

Near White River Junction

He loves me practically,
but I would have a shrine.
Four small new birds
with their mouths so wide open
lack   the nest hidden
here outside on the sill of this room.
He loves me practically,
but I would have a shrine,
not a robin's nest—
exit that idealized blue.
I cannot fix on recipes
as my friends do,
bitter greens   the things
that can't be said   a white room,
white tub that shines,
a vacation house
half-rinsed green from vines
close at the windows.
My marrow, it should be
teeming with mass and the made;
I feel it opening
to call its emptiness out.
I need a shrine.
A matter of votives   constant
lap of devotional waters, water-
lilies to suggestively wax
to me   to forget
each meager spring, indifferent
to need or worship.
And he walked away:
I have wanted someone to burn for me.
He walked away—night outing,
smell of sap at work on the dark,
an offering.   Sweetly it could boil up,
could quickly catch fire

this season could be that other
lost season
and I, one of the minor deities.

Already the Heart

The spinal cord blossoms
like bright, bruised magnolia
into the brainstem.
            And already the heart
in its depth—who could assail it?
Bathed in my voice, all branching
and dreaming. The flowering
and fading—said the poet—
come to us both at once.
Here is your best self,
and the least, two sparrows
alight in the one tree
of your body.

The Possible Man

for Vic Fitterman
and for my sister on her wedding day

For years the drops of belladonna in our eyes,
pupils poison-wide with devotion.

We lived on a black acre changing hands
in a room which seemed to say, "my love
is here" or "my love has just left."

And the aphrodisiac eels astir
in the bathtub, the dove's brains, fennel,
a musky glass of cognac.
We were the nightly part of a dictatorship.

When he sat slicing oranges, revealing
the hidden system, one after another, intricate
glistenings, eight and ten oranges, pure wet
color in a bowl, we said to ourselves
"he is a genius"—
                        in our confusion
we said it again when he ate them—juice
running, rinds like paper boats on the carpet
all as he pictured us,
the wide open white plywood bodies
on the firing range
and all of that shining blood.

Do we ever truly escape, then,
to this lazy stroll through the Luxembourg Gardens
its sweet boredom of forget-me-nots
small sailboats and fountain,
to the plainest of moments
with our husbands?
                        In sleep we hear them—
our possible men—"that's right"
"that's right" is all that they say.

And when will they call our names,
the new name, enticing us away
from a beautiful terror?

A Nectar

The girls have come into the shade
>   beneath the lilac's sharp heart leaves
>   beneath the canopy of minute Cécile Brunner roses
>   bewildering pink
with skirtfuls of honeysuckle.

They hold their skirts just so:
>   slack, as though waiting—a lifetime
>   of waiting and preparedness
>   to catch the person falling into them

Too precious you might say.
But their lives have slight torments
already. And adventures.

One of them has caught on fire.

They have watched swallowtails die
into a brother's collection
and lost money in the dark earth,
hidden profit from a lemonade stand—
their fingernails tight with dirt.

Judge, then, the girls' quiet
>   or what is most secret
>   within the secret of them

as they pinch off each pallid end, pulling
the stamen steadily, intent. They attend

>   to what you would only call
>   the small domesticity of the moment

>   to what spreads on the tongue
>   how it will be of use

Limbic

It was not only me, my
life marred by the shot

as he found all of himself
and ended it, startling the grouse.

A shot that registered
in the wild eyelid's snapshot

in the limbic jolt, the rapid shift and settlement
—one movement—further into camouflage.

The woman, too, with a toothache
trying to walk it off

stopped near the firehall,
and the kickback sound of it

here and there in the pines
moved in her ear and became her,

the fog or dusk already beginning
their memories of him,

the one just now fallen
from a shape in them.

We react.
My lover will open the book and find himself

front and center in a fame of sonnets,
how will he stand it? what will bolt or stir?

The blood begins.
It stains the wooden picnic table's bench

and which insect or animal
in the cold was drawn to it,

the night moving itself on,
making room for another.

The heron pulled its neck in,
labored skyward.

The deer looked up as deer will do.

Home Truths

Each clock in my house labors at its own maddening
time a few minutes or quarter hour north or south of the other
in a next room, and all spring the poor robin all day
on nest and eggs—what must she be thinking, hunched,
circling of twigs and warmth and *soon*
all the mouths wide. The historic side of the crib
lowered down. Raised up, each of the five children, super-
imposed, the stutter of all those first steps,
cakes and balloons—and between:
my father's version of home movies: sweet unpopulated slow
slow sweep the Grand Tetons or Crater Lake's eerie turquoise
          panoramic
Old Faithful the background click click click of grandeur
Half crazed he was an Ezra of tirades and theories—
transient goods luxuries   jerry-built houses   fakes   battleships . . .
I see now the geography of his peace in a family album
its several pages full (his first trip to Europe) cloud banks
each black and white photograph bisected by the dull purity
of an airplane's wing (and wing and wing and wing) the exact
          angle
of awe, his arrival above and in the cumulus:
a wide silence: majestic—   these golden
apples of the Hesperides.

Overture

There had been a cricket in the basement
when I dreamt you were an unopened envelope on my chest.
I heard on the radio how silverware suddenly tarnishes in a drawer
before disaster, tornadoes, sudden changes in weather.
The voice on the radio, on the lookout, she said, "It's beautiful...
it's not dark...it's good." Meaning the silverware.

For weeks we watched your heart
your breath, dip and peak and wander along the screen.
The week we brought you home, they found the long-gone
missing woman's body while deerhunting in one of the western
counties under the year's first snow.
   —every valley shall be exalted.

The television vet spoke of the terrier—jealous
and swallowing its owner's jewelry whenever she left,
even her dreamed-after diamond tennis bracelet.
I saw a bee-bearded man, listened to Tchaikovsky's span of months
and to a piece of music called the "Silken Ladder Overture,"

and just as finely were we ascending to some place past
the blurred coming-home-from-the-hospital photograph, beyond
even sight of our selves. I dreamt someone asked
for a lock of *my* hair in a world of perfectly
cloned sheep, of "silver needles" tea beneath

the all-throated prize finches. A blood and primrose world,
my darling, a white-tea-of-leaf-buds world, mild as your first tears.
When you sleep beside me, my arm locks across you.
O, how we'll whirl and circle, be whirled and fear-throated
a breathless carnivalesque, a ride of spinning-cups.

Peking Robins

At night you wake, not to seek me
but to come to your self, a small song,
here is your hand on the wall
in the squares the porchlight makes.
You are the day's hard rain. It becomes you
(and all the clouds in the pond).
Tonight the fox is struck, the steeple
reaches up but does not shine.
The town clock continues as your familiar.
Midnight and you wake, become the Peking Robins
restless from perch to perch at the bird shop.
You in tissue stained glass hanging darkly
centered in the window. You are that decoration:
the paper plate, its glittered rim, its glittering rim.

The Sears & Roebuck House

for Ken Ingels

The child in the atmospheric elm-dark of the parlor
has spelled a little word with lettered blocks:
ALL.
        The print had been small
in the catalogue
with its promise—vast numbers
of beautiful completed
houses, the millwork, the lathing,
one large attic.
The mother puts her hands in
to the wrist
in the dish sink: warm water,
the clouds mark a way across sky.
She thinks of all these houses
suited for the city, the town; the farmhome
ready-made. How situated
and accomplished. The pallets, the very walls
arriving by train. And the Newark stove.
Dear tidiness of structure.
That it suffice—what's sound and sure—
sound of the bronze and strike,
the one good knife for fixing supper.

Horde

This autumn you learn about the vertebrae in the cervical spine.
Which one has evolved to keep the heavy head up. There is a
      muscle behind
the scapula that, although large, is so thin it could hold a secret
in the circuitry of breath. The needles go in, the hope all along
your shoulder blades, daily experimentations,
and you could turn to the *hope-is-the-thing-with-feathers* thing.
Lithe, aligned and light, sketched into a bodily pleasure.
Now you must come, too, to a new understanding with your
      hands. Trying
to soften the Telemann; or the simple demands
of an F-major scale again. Hands dulled by misuse when they could be
undulant, swift-darting like the squirrels that hasten and how
to learn another way. There is one week when the burning bush
at the back of the house so catches the sun the guest room
is a red like the inside of an obsessive idea. And then the burning
bush is done—you wonder whether the room's conflagration,
that lit frenzy, was it actual or just that strange continuation of
      a sweat
that soaked your shirt through. You forget the glorious transit
of a common guest room, the wild California field burning in
      your burning
dream wicking closer to the mare in the pasture. So when the
      chimney-
sweep says it's lucky you had the chimney cleaned when you
      did—the sound
of a chimney fire is like an inbound-train—it's another day
      mid-life,
and you do feel the good fortune of all the lovely ways
      you've been spared.

VII.

NINE SKIES

Andrew Hears the Voice of His Own Elegy

I watch the candle flame, long in the spoon
as the room resounds with all
       that my brothers and sisters do not know.
  They think this meal will bring me back
to them. They ask what would I like
    and pass me bowls, full and steaming.

  All the love-ridden afternoon they gathered in.
Careful pictures were taken.
      As the shutter flicked its pale lid,
  I felt the hand on my shoulder
and looked off over my brother's head,
    his body there like a sorry shield.

  Catching the football, taking each clean spiral
deep in my lungs, I saw them
      wanting it to fall like some heavy joy
  finally come into my life, into my arms.
A sudden flock of birds interrupted
    the last pass into evening.

  Each face turned slowly, wishfully up.
Didn't they hear a wild sound
      chip the faltering sky? Or did the flock
  remind them of a young man writing home
from the Galápagos of feeding Darwin's finches
    green pepper, orange peel and chocolate?

  They must have imagined, reading the letter,
air stirred with amber and scarlet.
      But the finches were dull-colored: dun,
  mostly, and black. They didn't eat what I'd cast,
instead scattered with their myriad, famous beaks
    back to the scrub, to the hot, black ground.

I remember now how the air closed in.
How what they don't know will hurt
        soon: they'll dream over and over the .38's
    chill zero approaching the very temple lit
now by the candle's flame. I could have killed them—
    they'll know that instead I left them to live

with the finches always in the air behind them.

Motion Study

At dusk in the top bunk your plastic squadrons approached.
With decal snarls, they hung from the ceiling from invisible threads—
dim silhouettes, countless old war movies, the quiet onslaught.

Black Lionel locomotives shone poised on the shelf
—trackless—without the morse of their oily, false smoke.
Your room a secret terminal, the motion beginning.

You studied each constellation stalled on your wall,
the varied wings of your insect collection: moths tidily pinned,
cobalt dragonflies, thoraxes striped like fuses.

Lying on the floor one afternoon, you pulled rubber bands taut,
shot down each swaying model airplane. You perfected the whining
fall and the throaty sound of their exploding.

All through the evenings your wrenches hurriedly rang
the cement; the car rocked on its blocks as you raced the engine.
Legs forked out on the ground like a divining rod.

from beneath your Austin-Healey's shining flank,
you completed the apprenticeship,
saw in the sooted heavens how all along you'd been

greasing the gears of your own departure.

Passage

We with love will proudly hoist
those tatters made whole, so tailored for speed.
—Andrew Christie

My hand on your shoulder, I touched the end.
Your legs were drawn in. I saw the rim of underwear
above your pants; your jacket had shifted up, and there
was the taut and hollow spot below your last rib;
full-blown, your head in a bag like I throw my garbage in.
I think I could have withstood seeing whatever hint
of jaw or proud cheek held. And so, on this train,
fleeing from afternoon into evening—in a place
where you never were—you draw near, you begin.
Clouds move off on the wind, the train stirring up a trail
of turning leaves. A man whispers plans for the evening
in his lover's ear. A strand of her hair lifts on his breath.
A woman paints her lips a deep and deeper red.
In overheard conversations I hear more loudly the names
of places where you've been. I look at pictures of the Galápagos
and say to myself, his steps are still somewhere in the rocks,
his handprint still somehow in the whorled shell of the tortoise.
Like the professor—the Thoreauvian—who as a young man
uprooted a sapling from the edge of Walden Pond
and planted it on his own land in Halifax, Vermont. Like him
who lives on in that tree, you intervene in my bones, my joy
will be half yours. We pulled back our hair, cut a lock
from the nape to be burned with you, our necks pale
with January. When Ron Calder, the man who found you
on the playing field, said we didn't have to worry
about your having been out all night, all I could think of
was how cold and quiet it must have been. I imagined rain
pooling in your ear. But he meant that no animals had come
out from the pines to get at you. I see a blur of trees
from the train. They slow: each stop is just where we left it—
Laurel, Savage, St. Denis—I see the school. On the field
cheerleaders are still practicing. Their slender arms
make circles in the air, small angles; their skirts flare

as they jump. I think she was a cheerleader. In shadow,
the two of you shifted and bloomed like underwater things
in your old De Soto, spray-paint clouds down the sides. I try
to remember days at a time, but all is still about you.
You do a chin-up to the bar in the doorway or the splash
before you in the water turns to glass; you look at me
through the tension and pause of your thoughts. You skip
rocks out across the lake while over in the hills above Westbank
the planes leave streams of pink falling toward the fire.
Coming out from beneath your car, you hold a greasy bolt
to the light like a jewel; you sit in the dark, drag hard
on a cigarette, alight in the passing minutes with your own breath.
When I began the journey back to my coast after your death
I watched out over the Cessna's wing as the peninsula receded,
as the waves incessant off Point Roberts changed to a still,
grey blanket. So changed did the world seem to me
that I expected to see out my window row houses caving in
one by one all down my street, like the slow-motion footage
of earthquakes or a city's warehouses wired with explosives,
walls dropping away and the dust rising. I expected disaster,
a turbulent weather, to see just the marble steps left—the climb
to nowhere—trees uprooted, cars blown one atop the other,
their windows a violent Detroit lace. But there was no collapse.
The painters, suspended in their rigging, continued painting.
They whistled in the sun and one warm day, took off their shirts
and their muscles were beautiful, the chiaroscuro of grief
was beautiful. And finally, painstakingly, I made love to my husband
and it was for you, for all that you gave so suddenly away.
The croon of the train spreads into evening, light spills
before it on the track. The baby who wakes to every loud sound
sleeps through the whistle, and the woman's lost keys
have been returned by the conductor who tells her not to worry.
She had wondered how she would make it home. Daylight
is failing in the windows. Standard time: lights in the houses
come on. Maybe somewhere a brother tucks his sister
in a cardboard box with her blanket, pushes her gently
around the house. Maybe the girl pretends it is her coffin
and perhaps the brother, looking at her small hands,
thinks that living is enough. I remember the landscape

of plywood flat on two sawhorses. In the afternoons
under the mulberry, you and a friend set about making a world
for the train. You smoothed plaster over the fretwork
of chicken wire to make mountains; out of your cupped hands:
foothills. Each day further and further along—a resin stream
with flecks of tinfoil fish in it beside the tracks.
There was no city, just open, endowed land
which the train might traverse in ovals and come to know.
With your own hand you could make this world go wild:
whining speeds and grand wrecks on the turns. On the playing field
I put my hand in your blood. I made a handprint with it
on a piece of paper. I did not know what to do. I remembered
the many hands pressed into clay for Mother, your handprints
all over the bathroom, perfect in grease on the mirror, grey
on the soap. Your voice travels further into the distance.
Starting the long journey before us, you cut brush from the trails,
look back over your shoulder. You are like the sunken barge
in the lake. Dangerous, mysterious, we swim above you—
the sun is warm on our arms. We feel you in our bones
swimming over. But we come to shore, brush towels softly
against our necks, wrapped in our stories and myths.

The train eases into Camden Station, where men work
in the floodlights, building the new stadium. Dust they kick up
—caught in the light—makes their silhouettes barely solid.
I walk the platform. To the left: the old, block-long warehouse,
some 300 windows, a few of them bricked in, but always
the one light on in the one at the end. Pigeons wheel up
like newsprint into the rafters of the station: a quivering
sound as I walk home through the life you deepened.
Men gather round trash cans, rub their hands together, bonfire
full on their faces. How it drizzled day and night as the shock
wore off, a small fire snapping in the fireplace. I would walk
to the playing field and then deliberately back:
each step hard on the ground, the steps you did not take
and your dogs would run to meet me, the smell of woodsmoke
deep in their fur. How I used to blot up your wet steps—
brought inside from the lake—so the wood floors wouldn't warp.

And then there was no rain the day of your funeral. The Indians
say when the long rain ceases on such a day, there is no god
wanting to wash your footsteps away. Midnight off San Cristóbal:
you wrote home in the moon's wan light, the unknown stars
presiding. On your night watch you described dolphins
bringing you into harbor, the unmistakable sound of their blowing.
"They appear in an endless, dark water where phosphorescence
is great, trailing white light behind them," you said,
"their paths perfectly parallel and disappearing." The day before
my flight out, I found letters from your voyage, ran my fingers
over the words—passage, tortuga, *Birrahlee*, leeward, music—
felt their grip in the insubstantial paper. Then I came home
into my life, marked by you like the old table where your words
are still: backward, each syllable rough in the soft wood.

Your Harmonica

Their coming back seems possible
For many an ardent year.
—Emily Dickinson

The words I have spoken since,
the full breath in-drawn to the song,
a want-torn sort of aftercalling—
all part of the air from my lungs.
It croons in the slats, the blues
cupboards—shines, blurs its minor
whine through the slant-lit classroom
and the children making poems
shape its sharp, garish squall
into a candy apple. They raise
their almost translucent hands,
tell me it's like hearing San Francisco;
its brash glissando, the stirring
in a puddle the last rainy day
they remember. They close their eyes
to those darker dramas: the swoon
and blare of sirens
all the dissonant afternoon,
someone falling downstairs.
No, they hear in its warping tune
the last brilliant inch
of the silver-pooling sun going down.
There—behind eyelids, spelling words,
math problems, the imagination trembles
and yearns. The harmonica, flat
and cool now, in my hand,
is like a rock you'd skip past
the sunken barge and out toward Penticton,
a barge gone down
through dark legend: sea serpents, horses lost
swimming in from the island.
I hear, then, a deep blue,
just-past-midnight sound

of lights from Westbank mingling
in the water. I, too, picture something
sinking, I tell them. Something
we can't bring back up,
but something intact—like a voice
saying even just one thing we remember.

In My Dream

you live in the thousand rooms
behind the Medusa doorknocker. Verdigris spills
its shock of turquoise through her skull, twists
in the fist-held braids coiling into serpents.
When I knock, you turn more and more to stone.

You tell me the angels are following:
I hear their wings beat in your breath.
Turning your clothes on the line to flame,
you watch ash spiral up, catch in the branches
outside your window. *They were too heavy*, you say.

The moon flashes like a lure, gloves my hands
as I reach past its light to cover you.
The back of your head is gone: your skull a thick frieze
of angels chiseled deeply. You mutter in sleep:
what's rustling, dead pockets, black wings.

All afternoon you strip the oleander of leaves.
Such are the messages received from songs, an overlapping
of strings insisting. You send me the last leaf, enclose
a poem about how my hands, in the moon's white gloves,
settle in your dreams. They are a kind of invitation.

I am holding a mirror in my palm.
The streetlight shines from it in to her face
blooming with ruin. She neither leaves
nor speaks. Her bronze lips reveal nothing,
Already it is hard to make your heart move.

Midnight: a hollow sound, your piss
in the toilet too loud through the walls of my room.
I look out over the courtyard. All stone, you stand
in the fountain—the arc of water shining.
I toss my lucky coin and the house falls down.

Liberty Print

For my sister

Under the abiding lamp, appearances and disappearances;
the needle shines: up through the billow of pale hydrangea,
back down into daphne
small strawberry blossoms,
beneath the fragile green.

                    This fine cotton is tired and thin.
Each time I wear the blouse the strain pulls at the twilit wild rose
and morning glories fray along their immaculate edges.

You brought the Liberty cotton home
from your year at the Sorbonne, folded sharp-cornered
like handkerchiefs in your suitcase, to make each of us a blouse.

You spread the flawless cloth out on the table,
a rustle as you pinned the tissue pattern pieces down.

Yours also floral, warm-hued with slight yellows.

Mine was this fluctuation of lavender, half-sky and green
with a deep blue intruding from the background like a stain,
        an afterthought.

             You told me then as the shears hissed
how one evening in the café you'd tried to ask a man

when the Eiffel Tower's lights might come on. *A quelle heure
la tour s'allume?* you'd said.
                When would it be lit on fire?

This was long before we knew of danger.

                The pattern was easy to follow;
the pins shone, a cheerful path into the light.

~

The light shines in the eye of the needle I thread once again
to mend the frail seams ill-worn by a day's reaching.

I begin near the shoulder seam, the dark blue here
                        like a shadow, like midnight.

The lamp illuminates the patient stitches,
loops of purple thread, a collar pressed still
to its precise and thoughtful point.

You were sewing one afternoon—lost in a daydream—
needles and pins sharp from your mouth like a fish's whiskers.
When you swallowed one
                        we made jokes about how for eternity
you'd set off airport security systems.
                                    We were afraid.

The doctor never found the needle on the X ray.
At any time it could, like some shimmering pickerel, swim
through you, right to your heart.
            But it disappeared in a cushion of tissue.

This morning you mentioned the calm,
the woman putting one hundred needles into your skin.
            To help the grief, you said.

I imagined the needle stirring in you,
thinking it had come finally into the afterlife,
had rejoined a bristling host of the lost
in the quiet of your flesh.

And I thought what it would be like
                        —you and I, the rest of us—
that moment, seeing again the brother we lost
just a silent year ago.

After we hung up I took out the blouse.
The scissors caught like kindling in the lamplight
                              as I made the first, long cut
toward the first corner of a handkerchief.

Idée Fixe

As a child I made the bruise,
ornate, beautiful around my eye,
an afternoon's art, its fluctuate hues
equivalent to a hoarse, thwarted cry.
He once shone the flashlight up
into the suburban sky, my father:
this will go on forever.
He once opened the car door
so I could see the aggregate danger
blur by. And when that light returns
like the bateau mouche's blinding second,
its slowed sweep, I stand so white,
searchlit and still in the awe of testimony.

Late Swim

I leave the day behind in the churned light.
The water is sour in my mouth,
each accurate breath new, filled with citronella,
with oleander unfurling its poison in the dark.
        I turn and turn, want to reach you,
want you to dive silently in, rise under me,
clasp my ankle in your hand.
I can almost hear your slick, wet steps
Mother there near the tiki lamp
clipping dead roses heavy into a brown paper bag.

I turn toward the lamplight, swim
into the stutter and shine of home movies
where you paint your white way down a fence.
I hold still your smiling.
        You are lost in a flood of boys
down the steps of your first communion.
Strangely absent in the next frames, just your trout
arranged on the sand, jeweled and diminishing.

The dancers' kilts sway too quickly.
Under a tired sky they dance the sword dance,
        the fling, to your soundless piping.
Near Rushmore you turn to the camera.
I reverse the film: you back away
from the shadowed men, leap
from the aquamarine to the diving board:
the splash healed, I rescue you every time.

Spirit Line

...whatever has happened lies
beyond our grasp, deep down, deeper than
man can fathom.
—*Ecclesiastes 7:24*

Here the nighthawk's silhouette slurs and lilts
against a chalky twilight,
              above the one-after-another
tilt of row houses downtown.
                  At first
I thought he'd lost his mate, so fixed
was his circling and calling out over the same spot.
Everyday the telltale plummeting.

        What was it in the plains you saw ruined?
the buffalo's slow drift across the land,
its inevitable shadow
              one and the same as what
had its claim on you.

           What was it you reached for,
then, in the blackberry bush, leaning
from the ladder your whole body in,
you hands stained like someone wanting
                 to live.

When we laid you down, the eagle spread its wings.

Lifting above the cliffs,
            it cocked its white head
from some Indian legend where the eagle has the truth
—face to face with the sun but never blinking—
and a smaller flock of birds banked on the air and fled.

           On the wind
there is always, isn't there, the eagle-bone whistle,
its skirling and untranslatable message?

It sends your brother to a butte above the Snake River.
                    Or there he stands
in the cool, uneven, already interpreted
shadow at Devil's Tower.

                    You see,
even now, still, we are working this
into some elaborate design with little to go from.

We dye the wool wet with blackberry,
and watch as the nighthawk pulls its weft of cirrus through
to a selvage taut with feathers.

                         Trees, window frames,
the beams of our ceilings, the looms we are at work on,
looking up into the night's thick motif
    wondering where it is,
if there can be a place for your laughter.

And there is your younger brother
under the slow crab that moves ever sideways
                    through the black cancer sky,
memorizing the Snake River's starlit shape as it
meanders through the heartland.

He will bring home the pale warp of it.

It will be our spirit line,
like the weavers of Two Gray Hills worked in:
                    a sure path out to the border, an escape
from the middle of the hypnotic design.

                                        for Stuart and his brother

Coin

In the dark inside my skull rests a coin—
passage to the next world. The ferryman will take it
from under my tongue. As it warms in his palm
he will mint my body a rich future.

What hidden currency will help in this world?
To whom do I give the ruby-throated birds, breast-bound
and frenzied? my dreams lined with glittering Orion?
the answering song through the flute of bone?

I gather the snow's loose change to give someone.
I save air turned to coins in the frozen pond;
I save the pale moon where, in winter,
geese and swans fold their wings and shine.

Into the Solid Air

Ice fogs over water like cataracts,
casts shadows which join and dim.
Ascending into the solid air, three whales ram
the closed sky, heads covered in barnacles,
scarred with each attempt.

Do they remember the ease
of heaving those bodies into sunlight?

Caught in the one lit column,
in the trap of their breath, they rise
like belief to unleash skyward
a flawed and necessary mist.

They continue to search.
Where are the bounds of darkness?
Airless and far off that place
to cross into light.

Each night the news transports us
to that hem of ice
where, as winter seals them in,
something in us is opening long enough
for the pure struggle to be seen.

Their Titanic

for Zoe

In a dark theater, children startle at the stereophonic sound
of pressure, at the pale green water bubbling up
around them, at the sudden descent.
Could be the beginning of some bad dream
they can't put a finger on, pulling into night's
harbor all their lives long. The ocean goes dim
just as the lights filing in to this
large format field trip. So real we are reeling
back in time on the White Star Line, the insignia
a small flag, a twist of ribbon worn in the hair.
Back to the draft horses dragging the anchor
through the streets of Belfast, way back
into legend, a boatbuilder riveted into the hull.
We hear him calling, iceberg ice singing
in cocktails as the ship goes down. Isn't this almost
the size of our fear, eleven stories, that vast man-made
thing? The searchlight pauses on a banister
with a lyre design, on a stack of plates,
some upright tea cups skittering along like wan crabs
and then, all through the auditorium you hear them
recognize it: *Look, a shoe, It's a shoe, There's*
a woman's shoe, A shoe, A shoe, A shoe...
And in this exhaled apprehending, an ending.
They understand. The ocean they were pretending
was an untidy room it was now time to clean,
admits to the dark historic, the catastrophic
and, as their teachers have often reminded them,
this planet we all spin so slowly on is mostly ocean.
Now as they ride the bus home afternoons, the shadows
of clouds are terrifying, like a giant hand reaching for them.

Legend

Veuillez me montrer sur cette carte.

At a small table in the airport lounge, we held your money to the broad glare
from those observation deck windows, held it against the Boeing's shadows,
the comings and goings. We saw all the barely-there faces dim and changing
hands. And didn't they become, weren't they the ghosts we carry into the
wide world, the one maybe watching as we move on? You'd spend your first
few weeks in France lighting candles for him: a guttering, minute light to lick
the ancient dark of cathedrals. How the slender and pointed flame might look
like the first letter of his name there alone on your knees to this rapt
pilgrimage. And I'd read how Chartres, late in the twelfth century, burned
and burned. For three days, the leaden roof poured down onto the paving
stones. I was glad when you slipped their half-glances from beyond the
counterfeit back in your large wallet and unfolded the map instead like a
paper airplane. "Right here—across from the university," you said and we
looked for a place for you to swim in that quarter. I spoke the word
centime...centime, rubbing at the satisfying profile with my thumb. If you
couldn't think of the term for laundromat, your clothes might never get
clean—or so it seemed. All autumn, I waited for him at Drew's Laundry,
Andrew's Wash & Dry as though he'd come for his name, transparent on the
window, faint on the wall outside. I readied a trance of whites and delicates
turning over and over on themselves so he would step through the door, light
going awry. And I swam, the black-tile line trailing behind, like a jet's silent
tracing on the sky, for weeks what I'd seen—the sky's abiding feature—
looking upward this time, that time. Or maybe I followed the shadow of the
water's own remembering, the shadow of what the moon once put down on
its surface. Breath after breath, the outer world loud like a waterfall, the
clock sweeping round as the list of recordholders changed. And I knew you
were also swimming, trying to put some distance in the water behind you.
Before you left, we'd gone to the topiary gardens, each point of interest prim
and as neatly marked out as the arrondissements: the Keyhole, Water Lily and
Berry Gardens. Here the particular iris—even a scheme in the Wild Garden
leading us past the yew swans along the undulant hedge and into the plain
solemnity of the Great Bowl, right to the destined edge of the oval pool. That
night we listened in the dark to rain, something you'd not heard in a long
time; the electric storm never came as close as we wanted. Not long after
you'd gone, our childhood, oak-gnarled hills burned down to ash and the

heady scent of eucalyptus. Even now helicopters drop poppy and wildflower seed, great arcs of it into the charred wind and the thread-like roots of these slight flowers will begin holding the hills together as you sit quietly at the Tuileries, at the prow of Paris's own emblematic galleon—ghosts in your pockets and carrying on.

Darwin Crosses the Andes

All day we followed the *madrina* up into the mountains,
the steady rise and fall of her flecked, grey flanks tedious and hypnotic.
      The bell around her neck made a modest sound as each hoof
struck the terraced rock, our ten mules following
      their godmother, their long ears flickering to hear her.

During the ascent I felt in my chest the onset of the *puna*,
some small difficulty of breath. Many in Chile do not comprehend this.
      They think it is something in the rock, in the snow,
a power the mountains have. Truths will have their different origins.
      "These waters have *puna*," they say.

After the stubborn potatoes which would not cook
in the boil of this diminished atmosphere, "in the pot's iron curse,"
      I yearn to reach Mendoza where I hear watermelons are large
as a mule's head and a heaping wheelbarrow's worth
      of peaches, olives or figs can be had for threepence.

Climbing, I've collected thirteen species of mice.
What force is ever-tinkering with such variation?
      What is responsible for each splendid form, the lapses into ruin,
for the wild and profound? for the muddied torrents
      through these mountains, their furious inclination?

Tonight round stones borne end over end along the Maypu
make a hollow underwater sound, haunting above the roar
      toward the ocean. I hear in them time passing irrecoverably by.
My companions sleep through as sparks from the dry wood lift, torrents
      of brilliant lepidoptera in an extravagant sky.

Evermay-on-the-Delaware

You sleep in the sharp Adirondack chair,
surrounded by a still cloud of larkspur
and I am in the long shadows of lupine
which almost reach you in late afternoon.
I'm remembering the night of our wedding,
how rain throbbed on the windshield, each drop
a shadow blooming somewhere on the map.
I wanted you to know the way along
roads blurred by a fury of rain. I yearned
for you to reinvent yourself as lightning
spread its repertoire, its variations.
But love is each repetition, each small return;
night after night love is the way you gather
the birds, lifting their cage like a lantern.

Eye Brooch

The artisan fashions first the gold rims
of eyes hammered, narrowed to almonds, trims them,
thinks of what cluster of aquamarine,
emerald, pearl, tortoiseshell could suggest
the vast, refracted, heart-thirst of lust best
until they look on one another again.
How to craft all that such a want entails,
some discreet resemblance worn on her breast
or held, gazed on by a mistress until
she almost makes something of the heaviness.
What the encrusted eye cannot replicate,
nor the lover, is that something lost.
Deep, elsewhere, completely without shape—
desire just the chaos of its facets.

Alchemy

My body goes before me, like a lantern down a dark lane,
bringing one thing after another out of darkness into a ring
of light...My imagination is the body's.
—Virginia Woolf

In the dark morning you leave your empty cup on the counter
and after you've left for work I fill it again to continue.
I watch the milk swirl like a storm (although you take it black).
It is part of my same apprehending, the sound
of cardinals reminding me, long past a hesitant dawn,
just what world I've wakened to. And when I spend up until noon
in your heavy robe, use your toothbrush and pen and then pull
your turtleneck on, is it you I am trying to become?

I could turn to anything: laurel tree, reverberation, rain of coins,
swan...But I am more like the swans of Lohengrin, in Boston,
Lowell's swans, all wheel and pedal to move me
when someone sits down—a crude machinery. I have a friend
who wishes she had no body. How she could keep to herself.
A disappearance into pure mind: out beyond shadow, each touch,
each weightless wrong an irrelevance out past the dangerous.
Neither the drift nor pull, no going down on your knees.

And here I am busy with hiding, leaning my thigh to the radiator's
hot rungs, one version of a desire to have done with the body,
this grievance. The shadow of my breast no longer fine
but a place, you think, where my doubts rest and multiply;
and watch what used to be the simple path of your breathy promise
across the nape of my neck, how it catches in the swirl of hair there,
to you like some destructive curl on the weather map, replaying—
over then over—the shift of a certain vengefulness.

My body just some chart now of our impositions—an endless
navigation—or some diagram in a cookbook locating the prime
spots, the outline of the creature a convenience. And when models
in the magazines turn sideways and disappear, I am haunted
by the idea of that, the daydreamed after slick and glossy-aired,

paper-thin elision. If only to be clean for a single moment, something
pure and entire for you in a perfection of my own absence
like the calculated and empty gardens of Villandry

a precision along the Loire, its chalk banks giving off the stretch
of a day's heat into midnight. A still geometry, in relief some neat story
of desire. There a topiary maze of fans, hearts, masks, daggers.
Love's trimmed inconstancy. In the saccadic blur of this panorama,
this tidy cloister, the pulse and frill of ornamental cabbage:
on the perimeter a strewn lace of underthings. Swans moving
smoothly in the moats as though pulled on a string. There along
the angled design of a boxwood salon of pens and love letters.

No, I'll take the flawed clamor of the body, its wanting.
Like some letter written with lemon—the wavering flame will always give
me away, written all up and down. As night opens to its bewilderment
of heliotrope and rosemary, what is better than holding
the sweating glass to the temple, a slight lilt of chimes, the moon
turning my arm pale as a doll's arm, knowing what it is to be
out of breath, the water squeezed from the sponge at the collarbone,
the smell of the sun on you, knowing all of these exquisite threats.

Nine Skies

In the week when Tsao Wang who hangs
at the stove—the Kitchen God—leaves
for heaven to meet the Jade Emperor
he will speak well of us
for I have wet his lips each morning
with honey. His words will be sweet
as the litchi and he will have forgotten
our weekly misdeeds from the wine
I painted his lips with at night.

We will take him out and burn him
with the paper ladder I cut for his climb.
And we will watch him rise with our fortune
toward a new year, a pale smoke
I'll watch into sky—rising above
our backyard, over the bridge of magpies,
over the man across the street who kneels
painting characters, black and gold
good luck onto narrow banners.

I have already made the ladder,
cutting big squares from the paper—one
blowing out the window like a letter
sent far off. Right after I put the scissors
safe away in the drawer
where we will keep knives
on the long eve of New Year
so there will be nothing sharp
to cut away the good that might come.

We will pull at the chicken, the fish
kept whole to remind us of completeness,
of how two lives come together.
We will savor the fancy mushrooms
each of them like an opportunity.
And there will still be places at the table

set for those who have died, their chopsticks
perfectly parallel—their eight treasures pudding
sitting there before a vast quiet

of misfortune and the luck which took them.
Do not be sad in the year's first moments
you will say in the dark before bed.
I will take my luck money out
from the red envelope, walk careful
through the newness, the poised year.
And above the yard the last smoke
will dissolve like rice candy, or crickets—
a sound gone into the wind.

Notes

And I Began to Entertain Doubts:
This poem owes a great debt to Marina Warner's book *Fantastic Metamorphoses, Other Worlds: Ways of Telling the Self*; and to the article "The Girl Who Turned to Bone," by Carl Zimmer in the June 2013 issue of The Atlantic. Brief references to images or phrases echo Marianne Moore, Henri Matisse's cut-outs, Aristotle, Thomas Mann, and Louise Bogan.

Man Dragged by Horse, Tumultuous River:
The poem "On Longing" takes its title from a book of the same name by Susan Stewart and engages with her discussion of nostalgia and miniatures. "Ice Man" pulls details from various scholarly articles about the discovery and study of Otze, a Copper Age ice mummy found in September 1991 in the Otztal Alps. "Decline": *Departure of the Poet* is a painting by Giorgio de Chirico. "Man Dragged by Horse, Tumultuous River" is the title given a Mexican ex voto from 1920. Ex votos are small, primitive artworks—most often Italian or Mexican—with detailed visual and verbal narratives. They are left in churches by people in deep thanks to Saints and other Christian divinities for miracles and solutions bestowed on their families. Frida Kahlo's painting "The Suicide of Dorothy Hale" mimics traditional ex voto compositions. "Niagara" mentions several syndromes which come from essays on neurological anomalies by Oliver Sacks. "Amish Country" is dedicated to five Amish girls who were murdered and 5 school girls who were wounded in an Amish schoolhouse shooting in 2006, in Pennsylvania.

The Wonders:
The Seven Wonders of the World: A History of the Modern Imagination by John and Elizabeth Romer was of substantial help to this poem.

Little Surrender:
"Foreword": Eliot's phrase "female stench" was eventually struck from the Fire Sermon section of "The Waste Land"; I came across it in the facsimile edition of the poem edited by Valerie Eliot. "Winter Afternoons": the thinking about fairy tales echoes an idea from Peter Allenberg's *Telegrams of the Soul*. "Willingly" owes a debt to Leaping Poetry by Robert Bly. The title of this volume is taken from Sonnet lxxii in Edna St. Vincent Millay's 1931 book *Fatal Interview*.

The Housing:
"Already the Heart": Rilke is the poet, and the image of the tree is originally from the Upanishads. "The Possible Man" – "my love is here" or "my love has just left" came from an article on decorating that appeared in *The Baltimore Sun*. "Home Truths" – transient goods … battleships comes from a passage of Ezra Pound's quoted in Lewis Hyde's book *The Gift*. "Overture" – *Every valley shall be exalted* I hear as a line in the third aria of Handel's *Messiah*.